5X(9/09)5/11

5x (9/09) √3/13

MIRA MESA BRANCH LIBRARY
8405 NEW SALEM ST.
SAN DIEGO, CA 92126-2600

JAN 17 1996

Last Copy

D0786362

JAN 17 1996

MARGARET MURIE

A Wilderness Life

St. Lawrence
Island

Nunivak
Island

YUKON RIVER

Alaska

● Fairbanks

Canada

Kodiak

Gulf of Alaska

Earth *Keepers*

MARGARET MURIE

A Wilderness Life

Jennifer Bryant
Illustrated by Antonio Castro

SAN DIEGO PUBLIC LIBRARY
MIRA MESA BRANCH
JAN 1 7 1996

Twenty-First Century Books

A Division of Henry Holt and Company
New York

3 1336 03900 7605

The author thanks the following for their help in locating information:

The University of Alaska, Fairbanks; Diana Kodiak at the Elmer E. Rasmuson Library; the Margaret Murie Collection at the University of Alaska, Fairbanks; Mary Mathune at the Wilderness Society.

Twenty-First Century Books
A Division of Henry Holt and Company, Inc.
115 West 18th Street
New York, NY 10011

Henry Holt® and colophon are registered trademarks of
Henry Holt and Company, Inc.
Publishers since 1866.

Text Copyright © 1993 by Jennifer Bryant
Illustrations Copyright © 1993 by Twenty-First Century Books
All rights reserved.
Published in Canada by Fitzhenry & Whiteside Ltd., 91 Granton
Drive, Richmond Hill, Ontario L4B 2N5

Library of Congress Cataloging-in-Publication Data
Bryant, Jennifer
Margaret Murie: a wilderness life / Jennifer Bryant
Illustrated by Antonio Castro. — 1st ed.
p.   cm. — (Earth keepers)
Includes index.
Summary: A biography of the conservationist, known as the "godmother" of the environmental movement, who grew up in the Alaska territory and became a major force behind the preservation of the Alaskan wilderness.
1. Murie, Margaret E.—Juvenile literature.   2. Women conservationists—Alaska—Biography—Juvenile literature.   3. Environmentalists—Alaska—Biography—Juvenile literature.   4. Women pioneers—Alaska—Biography—Juvenile literature.
[1. Murie, Margaret E.   2. Conservationists.   3. Environmentalists.]
I. Castro, Antonio, 1941-   ill.   II. Title.   III. Series.
QH31.M926B78   1993
333.95'16'092—dc20 [B] 92-36289 CIP AC
ISBN 0-8050-2220-1
First Edition—1993

Printed in Mexico
All first editions are printed on acid-free paper ∞.

10 9 8 7 6 5 4 3 2 1

Contents

Chapter 1

The Great Ranges

The summer day is clear and bright in Grand Teton National Park. The big Wyoming sky is a deep shade of blue. A warm breeze sends a soft, quiet message through the valley.

Near the center of the park stands a sturdy log cabin. Margaret Murie, dressed in a cotton shirt and tan hiking pants, stands on the front porch. With lively, curious eyes, she looks at the mountain peaks in the distance. "If you keep looking at them," Murie observes, "you'll see that they never look the same way twice."

This simple cabin has been Murie's home for more than 50 years. Sometimes, when she looks up at the distant mountains, snow-covered even in the summer heat, she thinks of the great ranges in Alaska, where she lived as a child. It has been over 80 years since a nine-year-old Margaret first glimpsed the mysterious landscape of the far north. But she has never forgotten that moment. Margaret Murie fell in love with the quiet beauty of the Alaskan wilderness.

"All I can say now," she writes, "is that Alaska is indeed indescribable. Words cannot tell it. Pictures help— but they cannot convey the sense of space, the silence and the sounds, the sounds that belong there: bird song, wolf song, river song. And the air, the skies, the endless light of summer, the soft dark of winter."

Alaska is also a land of immense natural resources. Its history has often been the story of traders, trappers, miners, and loggers. It has been a story of gold and timber and oil. And too often, that history has been a story of carelessness and reckless abuse of the environment.

She also fell in love with a young wildlife biologist named Olaus Murie, and for almost four decades Margaret and Olaus shared their lives and their work. Together, Margaret and Olaus Murie fought to save the Alaskan wilderness from destruction and development. Since 1963, when Olaus died, Margaret Murie has fought on to preserve the beauty of a land that she calls "the last treasure of wilderness that we'll ever have."

Murie's work on behalf of America's wild places has been rewarded. In 1964, she watched President Lyndon

Johnson sign the Wilderness Act, which placed millions of acres of wilderness forest under the protection of the U.S. government. In 1980, President Jimmy Carter signed the Alaska Lands Act, protecting even more of the vast northern wilderness. She has also been rewarded by the countless young people who have been influenced by her work and her writings. A lifetime of effort has earned Margaret Murie a reputation as the "godmother" of the environmental movement.

Over the years, Margaret Murie has come to believe that "wilderness has a right to exist for its own sake." For Murie, the peace and beauty that nature offers are valuable natural resources, as valuable as the gold and oil that people have taken from Alaska for so many years. For Murie, wilderness has an impact on a person's spirit. It is, she says, a source of joy, of sensitivity, of happiness.

"Alaska must be allowed to be Alaska"— this is the call that Margaret Murie sounds. This is the conviction that has guided her life. It is a belief that Margaret Murie would like to pass on to future generations.

On this day, Murie turns her attention away from the lofty mountain peaks to the narrow, winding path that leads to her cabin. Today, as on many summer days, a group of young students from the nearby Teton Science

School follow that trail to receive a weekly nature lesson. "It's one of the most important things I do," Murie says. "Every time I see a troop marching up the path, I wonder how it will go, but I haven't had a bored look yet."

The students listen eagerly as Murie tells them about her early days in Alaska and about the many wilderness adventures she shared with Olaus and their three children. She shows them Olaus's collection of animal sketches and pictures from her family album.

They can see the plaque on the wall from the U.S. Park Service naming Murie an honorary park ranger. Over the door hangs a poster of the Arctic National Wildlife Refuge, nine million acres of Alaskan wilderness that Margaret and Olaus Murie worked to preserve. There are letters from senators and other members of Congress thanking Murie for her advice. There are letters from ordinary citizens, too, telling Murie how much they enjoy America's wild places and asking what they can do to help save them.

At over age 90, Margaret Murie is still active in the environmental movement, still concerned about the fate of the earth. She is hopeful about the future. "The young people I know give me great hope," she says. "They do care about what's left of the wild world, and they are willing to put their efforts into it."

"Every citizen has a responsibility toward this planet," Margaret Murie observes. "I'm counting on the new generation coming up. I have to believe in their spirit as those who came before me believed in mine."

"We had to depend on one another."

Chapter 2

A Young Pioneer

Margaret Elizabeth Thomas was born in Seattle, Washington, on August 18, 1902. Margaret's parents divorced when she was very young. Her mother then married Louis Gillette, an attorney. She describes her mother, Minnie, as "a sweet brown-eyed woman." Margaret's "Daddy" was her "loved and loving stepfather."

When Margaret (or "Mardy," as she was called) was nine years old, her stepfather was appointed assistant to the U.S. District Attorney in Alaska. Promising to send for Margaret and her mother as soon as he was settled, Margaret's stepfather traveled north by steamship, train, and horse-drawn sleigh. His journey lasted for more than a week and ended in Fairbanks, a bustling frontier town in the center of the vast Alaska territory. (Alaska would not become a state for almost 50 years.)

The United States had purchased Alaska (the Eskimo word for "Great Land") from Russia in 1867. It was a great land indeed: more than 500,000 square miles of treeless tundra, dense evergreen forests, inlets and islands, ancient glaciers, and giant mountain ranges.

Alaska is bigger than Texas, California, and Montana—the three next-largest states—combined into one. It contains the highest mountain, the largest glaciers, and the greatest number of active volcanoes in North America. The northernmost part of Alaska, where the land never thaws, lies within the Arctic Circle, at the top of the world. There, the sun disappears for more than two months during the long winter.

For most of the nineteenth century, the rest of America paid little attention to Alaska. Most people considered it foolish to have purchased this vast "icebox" at all. For three decades, the great northern wilderness was undisturbed, home to the Indian groups native to the region and to the hunters and trappers who made their living by selling the furs of Arctic hare, grizzly bear, wolf, beaver, and seal.

All that changed in the late 1800s, when gold and other precious metals were discovered near the settlements of Nome and Juneau. These discoveries attracted tens of thousands of people from the "lower 48" states, who left their homes and families to seek their fortunes in the north country.

With the coming of the miners, settlements sprang up to provide them with supplies and services. Fairbanks, located between two of Alaska's major mountain ranges, became one of the most important of these towns. There, Margaret's stepfather would establish his headquarters and attempt to bring order to a lawless frontier.

It was several weeks before Margaret and her mother received the telegram they had been waiting for: "Can you catch the [steamship] *Jefferson* on September 15th? Last steamer to connect with last boat down the Yukon. Will meet you." Margaret could barely contain her excitement. In less than two weeks, she would be in her new home in Fairbanks, Alaska.

For the next three days, the house was a collection of trunks and boxes. Margaret was sent racing to the dress-maker. "We're going to Alaska in three days," she shouted, "and Mother wants to know can you get her a traveling dress made."

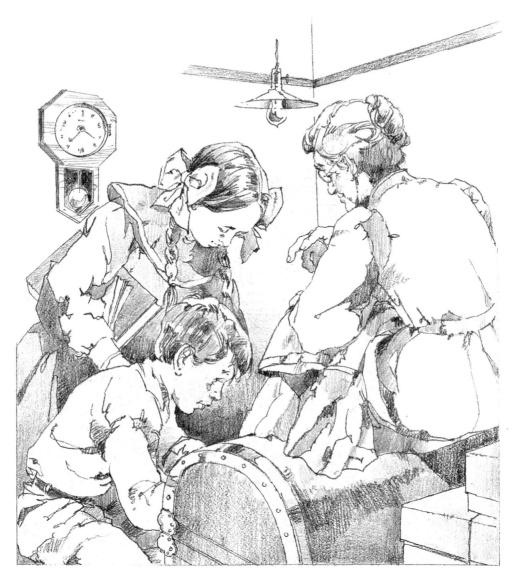

Margaret's grandmother came to help with the packing. Many years later, Margaret can still picture her grandmother "between tears and laughter, sitting atop the largest round-topped trunk so the dressmaker's son could get it closed."

Soon enough, it was time for them to board the steamer. A crowd gathered at the water's edge. In Seattle, going to the docks "was like going to the theater," Margaret wrote, "a real social occasion." Dressed in her best clothes and new shoes (they were "shiny black boots with patent-leather cuffs at the top and a red silk tassel"), Margaret squeezed her mother's hand tightly as they walked toward the giant steamship.

She smelled the salty sea air and heard the *Jefferson's* great engines churning and hissing. She remembers that her stomach was "tied in a knot" as they reached the red-and-white gangplank. "I was clutching all my going-away presents—coloring books, paperdoll books, crayons, a new volume of *Black Beauty*."

On deck, the passengers jockeyed for a spot at the ship's rail. As the last tie was cut loose, a hundred hands waved good-bye, a hundred voices shouted. "Tell Joe to write!" "Don't take any wooden nickels!" "See you next June!" The ship's whistle blew for the last time. As the ship moved out into the cool, black bay, the shore became a distant blur.

Margaret and her mother joined the other passengers in the *Jefferson's* lounge. "We children cut out paper dolls, and played Parcheesi, and colored pictures," she wrote.

Margaret enjoyed the sights and sounds of her voyage. On the fourth day, as the *Jefferson* prepared to dock at Skagway, Margaret stood silently on deck and studied the scenery. This was her first glimpse of Alaska. "We had been sliding for hours up a long channel of glass-smooth water edged on either side by the ever-present dark green forest that lay below shining white mountains," she wrote.

"A nine-year-old girl can see and hear a lot," Margaret Murie wrote. Although she spent a lifetime in the far north, her most vivid memory of Alaska remains "the one I saw first." She had found a new home in the Land of the Midnight Sun.

Following a good night's rest in Skagway, Margaret and her mother continued their journey by train. Margaret jumped from one side of the aisle to another, "trying to see everything," she wrote. Then, for the next stage of their journey, they took another steamship to the town of Dawson, where they were to meet Margaret's stepfather.

Margaret recalls standing on deck, searching for the big tan Stetson hat that her stepfather wore. "Squeezed against the white-painted iron mesh below the railing, new hat pushed askew, heart beating fast, I stood determined to see everything," she remembered. "Mother stood quietly beside me, but I could feel her excitement, too."

"There he is!" her mother cried out. That night, there was a happy crowd at Dawson's Arcade Cafe. And there was moose steak for dinner, a "huge, thick slab of meat."

The journey to Fairbanks continued again by steamship. For the children on board, it all seemed "a big happy game," Margaret said. "Life was almost more interesting than one could bear." Another train took Margaret and her parents to Fairbanks, where a horse-drawn cart brought them into town. The three-week journey was at an end, and Margaret was home.

Her new home was a log house at the edge of town. It was, Margaret noted, "the last house on the last street of Fairbanks of that year." There were only four rooms and a small shed that served as a bathroom and a storage area for wood.

Margaret's stepfather was soon called away to another part of the territory. He would be gone for several months. Margaret and her mother spent most of that winter trying to make their rough cabin-house more livable.

They soon discovered that life in this icy frontier was much different from what it had been in Seattle. "The thermometer went down to minus 20 and 30 and 50 and sometimes stayed there for weeks," Margaret recalled. Staying warm was a constant challenge. Margaret remembered that her mother's feet were always cold: "She would go busily about her housework for a half hour, then open the oven door and sit with her feet in the oven for a few minutes, then back to work."

For Margaret, the challenges of life in Alaska were simply part of a great frontier adventure. But for her mother, pregnant with Margaret's first half-sister and a world away from friends and relatives, it was a difficult adjustment. "I think my mother felt the unspeakable isolation more than she would ever say," Margaret wrote. "She kept it locked away inside, while she went about the task that was hers."

Margaret enjoyed growing up in Fairbanks. Most of the Fairbanks youngsters had a dog and a sled. It was in this way, riding behind her Husky, "Major," that Margaret became acquainted with the town and its people.

And what a town it was—"a flat patter of hodgepodge buildings and low log cabins," wrote Margaret, "smoke plumes rising straight up from all the little iron stovepipes defying the cold and loneliness and all the powers of the unbeatable North."

The miners and their "gold-seeking doings" were the heart of Fairbanks, the basis of the town's economy. But soon after they staked their first claims, they were followed by grocers, bakers, butchers, hardware merchants, and saloonkeepers. It was "a colorful tapestry," Margaret wrote, "woven of man's yearning for wealth."

The miners and trappers pampered Margaret and her playmates. There were so few children this far north. "They were a symbol of everything that most of these men had given up in heeding the call of gold and adventure," Margaret said.

Sometimes, Margaret and her friends gathered at the station of the Northern Commercial Company to watch the big "Yukon sleds" glide in with their load of supplies, visitors, and news from home. The company owned a fleet of horse-drawn sleighs that relayed goods and passengers from "the Outside." Their main route was the Valdez Trail, a rough wilderness road that connected Fairbanks to the southern port of Valdez. Even though the nearest town took eight days to reach, Margaret and the rest of the Fairbanks residents regarded the trail as "the lifeline to the outside world."

The rhythm of life in the far north, linked so closely to the changing seasons, was reflected in the daily activities of adults and children alike. From November to mid-January, the sun remained almost hidden, and temperatures could drop to 50 below for weeks at a time. Clothes could not be dried outside; they would freeze almost immediately. According to Margaret's diary, waking up for school was the hardest part of a winter day:

> Thirty below zero this morning. Frost has crept through the walls and caused the bed clothes to stick to the wall on that side, and it is agony to crawl out of the warm nest in the center of the bed when Daddy calls. . . .
>
> Barely a tinge of pink down in the east when my friends Irene and Lily and Marguerite come by for me. They have already walked four blocks and their faces and scarves are framed in frosty white. We all learned to be fast walkers, growing up in Fairbanks.

But there was ice skating and dogsled racing when the winter weather was right. Children learned to make their own excitement, Margaret noted.

The sun returned in February. The days lengthened slowly. By April, the snow began to melt, offering new opportunity for adventure. Now it wasn't so hard to go to school: "In late April, we school children are having

adventures every morning on the way to school, with huge puddles of water and slush to wade in and sail chips of wood on, to build make-shift bridges of planks across." One day, the announcement rang through the town: "The crocuses are out!" School was canceled for the day, and everyone hiked up into the surrounding hills to eat sandwiches and pick wildflowers.

In the warm months, hiking was Margaret's favorite activity. "I just liked to be outdoors. I'd go out by myself and wander around, so much so that my stepfather sometimes claimed I was part gypsy." Margaret welcomed these times alone in nature. "Somehow the quietness sank right into me," she later said. "I think it gave me strength."

Summer was "a glorious season," wrote Margaret, "in spite of the mosquitoes." To avoid being bitten by the annoying insects, children smeared their bodies with citronella (an oily substance that repels insects) and wore headnets and long sleeves when playing outside. Tennis matches and baseball games went on all day—and often all night as well during the period of time when there was sunshine 24 hours a day.

During the Fourth of July celebration, there were three days of parades, carnivals, and dances. For one holiday parade, Margaret was dressed up as the Statue of Liberty. "I had a tinsel crown and a 'torch' and felt terribly important," she recalled. She could never forget the tug-of-war contests between the burly miners, "the straining, bulging muscles, the grunted commands of the captains, the clenched teeth, the grimaces, the breathless tense silence of the holiday crowd."

Margaret Murie described the Alaska that she discovered as a child as a world apart from the rest of the world—a place of joy and hardship, of loneliness and friendship. "We were all far away from the rest of the world," Margaret wrote. "We had to depend on one another."

Chapter 3

A Sunrise of Promise

Despite the hardships that accompanied their move
to Alaska, Margaret's family prospered—and grew. In the
seven years that followed the family's arrival, Margaret's
two half-sisters, Louise and Carol, and her half-brother,
Louis, were born. The town of Fairbanks was growing,
too, with the arrival of hundreds of new families. Nearly
every household now had electricity and a telephone.
Margaret's mother found new friends among the members
of the numerous civic groups that served the community.
Margaret's stepfather was joined by two assistants in the
new courthouse on Cushman Street.

Margaret was now 15 years old. Because there were
no colleges in Alaska at the time, her parents arranged
for Margaret to attend Reed College in Seattle. Margaret
described herself as "shy, yet eager for adventure—scared,
yet determined to go ahead."

It was the spring of 1918, and a new era was about to dawn for Margaret—and for the town of Fairbanks. The Northern Commercial Company had announced its last run on the Valdez Trail. Soon, there would be a new railroad stretching from Fairbanks to the southern cities of Seward and Anchorage, replacing the long-established relay of horse-drawn sleighs.

"It had turned out that I was to be the one to go over that mysterious trail on the last trip," Margaret wrote. "I was trying to act as though it wasn't very much. Actually, of course, I felt I was the favored one of the whole universe, at the same time wondering how I could possibly leave behind Mother and Daddy."

Just before midnight on May 4, Margaret's father took her to meet the sleigh. The driver was Roy Rynearson, whom Margaret remembers as a "stalwart and good-looking" man, with "twinkling blue eyes in a face burned to leather by the spring sun reflecting off the snow." At midnight, Roy hoisted Margaret up onto the wolfskin-covered seat and pulled away. The thought of leaving her family and friends frightened Margaret. She tried to imagine "the unimaginable adventure ahead."

For the next five days, Margaret traveled through dense black-spruce forests, plunged down slippery creek

banks, crossed the melting spring streams—until the big Yukon sled took Margaret safely to the foot of the Alaska Range. A dogsled and two more sleighs brought her to the end of the trail.

After nine days, the journey was almost over. At the last stop, the driver picked two shiny silver dollars from the mud kicked up by his horse's hoof. "He wiped the coins off on his trousers and handed me one," Margaret recalls. "Keep this always, it's your lucky dollar," he said. "I'll keep this one for mine. Good luck."

For the rest of her life, Margaret would be able to say, "I still have that dollar."

At the end of her second year at college, Margaret again found herself on the Valdez Trail. But this time she was heading north, going home for a visit. And this time she was traveling by car. "Four days of bumpy, hilarious, stuck-in-the-mud pushing and shoving"—that's how Margaret remembered the trip home.

In the weeks that followed, Margaret reacquainted herself with her family and their neighbors. "I've got a new pal I want you to meet," one of her friends said to Margaret soon after her return. "His name's Olaus Murie, and he's with the Biological Survey."

Margaret and Olaus walked home together that first night. It was "a rosy northern evening," Margaret remembered, and this young man "was not like any of the rest."

A few days after their first meeting, Margaret and Olaus took a boat ride together. "We heard a great horned owl hoot far off in the forest," she recalled. "Olaus answered him. Again the owl spoke, a bit closer this time. Olaus hooted again, and so it went until suddenly out of nowhere the soft dark shape floated into a treetop right above us on the riverbank and sat silhouetted against the golden sky."

"What kind of magic did this man have?" Margaret asked herself.

The "magic" that Olaus seemed to have was the result of years spent developing the patience and skills needed to be a naturalist. Olaus Murie had arrived in Alaska in 1921 to study caribou herds. He was a government field biologist, a scientist who studies animals in their natural habitats.

His half-brother, Adolph Murie, also a famous biologist, remarked that Olaus "had a reputation in Alaska as a wilderness traveler, and it was well deserved, for no one was more tireless, both physically and mentally." A fellow scientist, George Marshall, once wrote that Olaus "could discover more in an acre than most of us see in many square miles."

But to Margaret, he was "a slim blond man . . . with the freshest complexion and the bluest eyes."

"How can he be a scientist and be so young?" she wondered.

In 1921, the year he met Margaret, Olaus was beginning his study of the feeding, mating, and migration patterns of Alaska's great caribou herds. Little was known about this cousin of the elk because the wilderness areas of northern Alaska were still largely unexplored. It was Olaus's job to observe and record the habits of the caribou and to collect specimens of their hooves, hides, and bones for further study in Washington, D.C. This information would help scientists understand the place of these animals in the vast Alaskan ecosystem.

Over the next year, the friendship between Margaret and Olaus deepened. She liked his calm and patient manner—he was a gentle man, but with steel within, she said. He admired her eager curiosity. By the following spring, they both knew that "there was no life for us except together."

Margaret decided to complete her college education at the newly established University of Alaska in Fairbanks. It was just the second year of the college's existence, and Margaret was the only senior among the 52 students. "What an eager, excited group we were!" wrote Margaret. "It is a special thing to be part of the beginning of something. Everybody had such hope for the university."

By the summer of 1924, Margaret and Olaus were engaged. But they were soon to be separated again, this time for five months. The Biological Survey was sending Olaus to the Yukon to study waterfowl. Wedding plans were made hastily before Olaus left. The couple decided to get married on August 18—Margaret's twenty-second birthday. The ceremony would take place at Anvik, a remote settlement on the Yukon River. Their honeymoon would be a wilderness voyage to the Brooks Range, Alaska's northernmost chain of mountains, where Olaus would continue his caribou study.

"You do want to go, don't you?" asked Olaus.

"Yes, I want to go," Margaret replied.

Nothing about this whole romance was ordinary, Margaret later observed. What could be ordinary about a honeymoon north of the Arctic Circle? Margaret's friends and family teased her as she prepared for her wedding trip: she packed a tent, a camping stove, a sleeping bag, snowshoes, wool socks, flannel pajamas, and a fur parka. "Not a dress, not a bit of lace or a ribbon," she noted.

The fact that their first weeks together as husband and wife would center around Olaus's work didn't bother Margaret. "That was one of the adjustments I had to make on our honeymoon," she said. "The work came first." Years later, Margaret described herself as "the bride who happened to be along on the collecting trip."

On June 13, 1924, Margaret became the first woman to graduate from the University of Alaska. "I was it," she couldn't help but point out. "I *was* the senior class." There was a big band to celebrate the occasion; even the governor was on hand to honor the university's newest graduate.

Two months later, accompanied by her mother and

her best friend, Margaret headed upriver on the sternwheel steamer *General Jacobs*. The plan was to meet Olaus downriver from Anvik, then take the steamer to the church. But the happiest day of her life was tinged with worry. "In all the five months since March, I had two letters and no recent word," Margaret wrote. Travel in the wilderness was always unpredictable. There was simply no way to know if Olaus would be there on time.

On August 18, twenty-two-year-old Margaret waited nervously in the stateroom of the *General Jacobs*. The day dragged slowly by until finally, just before eight o'clock in the evening, Margaret heard a cry from someone on deck: "There's Olaus! I see him!"

A wave of relief swept over Margaret. "All I could think of was how fast my heart was pounding," she wrote.

The wedding took place by candlelight inside the little log church at Anvik. "It was like a dream," said Margaret. After the ceremony, the newlyweds returned to the steamboat for the journey north. The sun was rising as they slid away from the shore, Margaret remembered. "Out across the wide gray river, over the low willows, there was a bright splash of rose and molten gold.

"A sunrise of promise," Margaret Murie called it. "A beautiful world was waking to light."

"I feel very comfortable in the wild country."

Chapter 4

Arctic Adventures

Heading up the Koyukuk River aboard the steamboat *Teddy H.* (Margaret called it her "ship of adventure"), the Muries watched the changing landscape. Though she had lived in Alaska for many years, Margaret wondered at the wilderness world they were passing through, a world so different from that of the frontier town. To Margaret, "it was like a dream world, so beautiful that there is hardly any way to tell about it." The couple spent their days in "a golden happy haze."

The steamer took them to Beetles, a remote Indian settlement on the Yukon River. There, they unloaded their supplies and moved into a big one-room log cabin. There was too much equipment for them to carry into the mountains on foot. Margaret and Olaus would have to wait for the river to freeze and the snow to fall so that they could "mush"—travel by dogsled.

While they waited for "freeze-up," Margaret and Olaus set up housekeeping. Their first meal in this world apart from the world was macaroni and cheese. For Margaret, it was a moment to treasure, a dream come true. "We had the warm light of a kerosene lamp on the table, the cheerful crackling from the stove; and to make it complete, as darkness fell the rain came, a soft patter on the roof, with a whisper of wind."

During their first week in Beetles, Margaret learned how to assist Olaus with his studies. "I learned where to look for mouse holes and feeding places and was shown their tiny runways, like an intricate street system for fairies," she wrote. "I learned that to the scientist these little creatures are interesting and important, for they have a relationship to bigger creatures and to the land and are part of the great chain of life."

Margaret Murie had received what she called her "first lesson in the importance of careful observation." She began to see the rich life of the Alaskan wilderness.

Margaret also got to know Fuzzy and Mally, Ungiak and Wolf, Mayuk, Bingo, and Pooto. These were the huskies who would lead Margaret and Olaus across the winter wilderness. In the weeks of hard travel that lay ahead, the Muries would rely on their dogs to move safely through a desolate and dangerous landscape.

When the river was completely frozen and enough snow had fallen, Margaret and Olaus set off for the mountains. It was, Margaret wrote, "a fine frosty day to hit the trail," twelve degrees below zero—just right for mushing.

Running behind the sled, Margaret quickly grew too warm. She threw back her parka hood, enjoying the crisp feel of the air. "How light my moccasined feet felt," she said, "padding along on snow-sprinkled ice at a dogtrot, every muscle responding to the joy of motion, running, running without getting out of breath."

As the sunlight began to fade that first day, they camped along the river. Olaus unhitched and fed the dogs while Margaret made dinner—a stew of rabbits and ptarmigan (Arctic grouse) which Olaus had hunted along the way. At last, they huddled together beneath the stars. The Arctic moon shone brightly over the silvery snow. A great horned owl "whooed" in the pines around them; an Arctic wolf howled from a distant mountain peak. From a nearby thicket, a hare silently scampered across the river ice.

A steady routine of mushing, camping, resting, and mushing again continued for nearly 10 weeks. On a good day, they covered many miles with what seemed like little effort. But on other days, when the weather was harsh and the bitter Arctic air stung their faces, travel was slow and wearisome.

Every day brought new lessons in the ways of the wilderness. As Margaret noted, often that lesson was simply the joy of sliding along on top of the world: "Days on the trail taught us that there is always and forever something to rejoice about."

After weeks of travel, the Muries at last made camp on a snowy mountain slope overlooking the caribou-speckled tundra. The next morning, Olaus left their tent to collect caribou specimens. He planned to send them back to Washington for further study.

Margaret stayed behind to finish setting up the base camp. When daylight faded and Olaus had not yet returned, she wondered what to do. In truth, there was little she could do. Margaret curled up in her sleeping bag to keep warm. But thoughts of danger were never far away from her imagination. And when Olaus finally came through the tent door, carrying a caribou head on his pack, he found Margaret sobbing wildly.

Margaret came to see that night on the mountain as another wilderness lesson. Being a field biologist's wife was not going to be easy. She would have to learn not to worry.

The caribou study lasted through November. As the Muries prepared to leave the Brooks Range, Margaret thought about how the wilderness trip had changed her. "If you're living in some untouched area, some wilderness, you just can't go off and forget it," she said. "It does something to you."

Margaret considered this "something" a kind of gift to the human spirit, a sense of well-being and wholeness. "I feel very comfortable in the wild country," she told her friends when they asked how it felt to be alone deep in the wilderness. "It's a very peaceful feeling."

By the time Olaus received his next assignment, Margaret was expecting their first child. She remained with her parents while Olaus completed a half-year study of brown bears on the Alaskan Peninsula. Margaret found the separation almost too much to endure.

When Olaus returned, they decided that Margaret and their new baby, Martin Louis, would accompany Olaus on all future field trips. Friends and colleagues could not believe their decision. "The wilderness is no place for children," they protested. "Little Martin would be safer at home." But the wilderness *was* the Muries' home.

Over the next several years, the family grew to include two more children, Joanne and Donald. True to their decision, the Muries raised their family wherever Olaus

carried out his field work for the government. "They grew and were brown and never had a sick moment that I can recall," Margaret wrote. "Their play was no problem: they were busy from morning 'til night with places and objects they found right in the wilderness."

In 1927, the Muries moved to Jackson Hole, Wyoming, near the Teton range. The government had sent Olaus there to find out why the largest elk population in North America was dying off. It was a very serious conservation problem.

After several years of studying the elk population near Jackson Hole, Olaus came to the conclusion that the growth of western cattle ranches had disrupted the elks' way of life. Ranchers had disturbed the balance of the wilderness ecosystem by killing off the elks' natural predators, such as wolves and mountain lions.

Also, the cattle ranches had claimed much of the elks' feeding ground, forcing them to move to less suitable areas where the vegetation was too rough. As a result, a large percentage of the elk herds had developed a disease called "sore-mouth," which, if infection set in, could be deadly. Olaus recommended that the National Elk Refuge be enlarged to ensure the future safety of the herds.

Such a recommendation would not be popular, certainly not with the region's ranchers and loggers. But the Muries knew that the wilderness areas they loved were in danger. Human interference could destroy the fragile balance of natural ecosystems. They knew that people had to work to save the wilderness. Margaret and Olaus were ready to join the fight.

In 1937, they joined the Wilderness Society, a newly formed group whose members were fighting to protect the remaining wilderness areas in the United States. When the society asked Olaus to join its governing council, he accepted with Margaret's full support. It was a decision that changed the rest of their lives.

Chapter 5

Sounding an Alarm

It was, Margaret Murie said, the age of the bulldozer.

After World War II, the growth of population and industry threatened to destroy what was left of America's wilderness areas. America was on the move, and the direction of that move was westward.

New highways, new housing developments, new shopping centers—a new generation of settlers placed their demands on the environment. Centuries-old forests were cut down to meet the demand for building materials. Rivers were dammed to create reservoirs for a supply of fresh water. Even the mountains were blasted with dynamite to clear the way for new roads.

In 1945, the governing council of the Wilderness Society asked Olaus to become its director, a position that would require his family to move to Washington, D.C. Knowing that they would never be happy in the city,

Olaus agreed to accept the job for half the usual salary if he could remain in Wyoming. The job was then split between Olaus and another field biologist, Howard Zahniser, who ran the office in Washington.

The change came at the right time for the Muries, who disapproved of the way the Biological Survey had been managing wildlife in certain areas of the country. In the western states, for instance, government employees routinely killed wolves, coyotes, and mountain lions, considered by ranchers to be "varmints." Olaus protested this practice and others like it that interfered with the natural balance between prey and predator.

Olaus left his government job to work on conservation issues. But it was not an easy adjustment for the Muries. Olaus and Margaret had spent most of their married lives in the wilderness, raising their three children and carrying out field work for the government. They had moved to Moose, Wyoming (part of Grand Teton National Park), and now their log-cabin home was the scene of a different kind of work.

The Muries sought to sound an alarm so that people would wake up to the environmental dangers facing the American wilderness. Though Margaret called herself Olaus's secretary, she was really a partner, contributing equally to the struggle that seemed to have taken over their lives.

The Muries had become an important voice on behalf of the wilderness. They traveled throughout the country for the Wilderness Society, giving lectures on the importance of preserving wildlife habitats and saving endangered ecosystems.

The Muries attended government hearings, supporting new legislation that offered protection to wild areas or created a new national park. Whenever an established park or wildlife refuge was threatened by development, the Muries fought to save it.

One such case occurred in the early 1950s. The government wanted to build a dam on the Colorado River where it flowed across the Utah border. This area, known as "Echo Park," was part of Dinosaur National Monument, which had been protected from development since 1915. In addition to rare deposits of dinosaur fossils, the region included a hundred miles of canyon wilderness. A dam would supply electricity to the area's homes and businesses, but at the cost of flooding these ancient canyons.

The leaders of the Wilderness Society and other environmental groups fought to stop the dam. It took years of work to convince enough members of Congress to vote against the project. But in 1956 the Echo Park project was defeated.

There were many other battles. During this time, the protection of Alaska's wilderness regions became a national issue. The Alaskan Highway linked the territory to the "lower 48" states, and the airplane had made transportation to and from the region more efficient, opening up Alaska to more and more people. Conservationists were convinced of the need to preserve large areas of the Alaskan wilderness before it was too late. Also, there was growing support for Alaska to become a state. What would happen to the wilderness of the far north when the federal government was no longer in charge?

Beginning in the mid-1950s, the Muries launched a campaign to have a national wildlife refuge created in the northeastern section of the territory. Bordering on the Arctic Ocean, such a refuge would cover several million acres, including the calving grounds of the caribou herds that Margaret and Olaus had followed on their honeymoon. The annual southern migration of the herds—more than 170,000 animals—was one of the greatest wildlife spectacles in North America. The proposed refuge would also protect the habitats of hundreds of other wild animals— moose and wolverines, waterfowl and shorebirds, oxen and wolves, foxes and bears.

To support the establishment of the refuge, Margaret and Olaus returned to the Brooks Range, this time traveling by plane. They surveyed the area and collected information to convince the government that the region should be permanently protected. The trip, Margaret wrote, "only wedded us more strongly to this beautiful independent world, with all its natural living going on around us."

The government held several public meetings to debate the issue. "There is a great gift to be won in places like the Arctic Wildlife Refuge," Margaret Murie explained.

"Alaska is the last treasure of wilderness that we'll ever have," she said. "I think we need to be very careful about what we do with it."

Their conservation work kept the Muries busy. But that work only seemed to enrich their lives, to give them a sense of purpose and accomplishment. "It was the best time," Margaret later recalled. "It seemed that our lives just blossomed."

In 1959, Alaska became the forty-ninth state. The following year, on December 6, nine million acres of Arctic territory were set aside as the Arctic National Wildlife Refuge, the largest wildlife refuge in the United States. The Muries heard the news by telegram the next day. "There's wonderful news," Margaret announced, as she presented the message to Olaus. "Olaus was at his table at the back of the room, writing. I held out the telegram to him; he read it and stood and took me in his arms and we both wept."

For years, Margaret Murie had made a habit of keeping a diary whenever she was in the wilderness. By 1960, her personal writings covered several decades of her life. A friend of the Muries, who was also a publisher, suggested that Margaret write a book about her Alaskan childhood and her travels with Olaus. In 1962, Margaret's first book, *Two in the Far North*, was published. It captured the frontier flavor of her childhood in Fairbanks, her unusual wedding and honeymoon, and many of her wilderness adventures.

This time of success and satisfaction was soon overshadowed by deep sadness. Olaus had been struggling with cancer for years. Despite several operations, his condition worsened. Olaus Murie died in 1963.

"I can't do it," Margaret Murie said to herself when she came home alone to the cabin at Moose. "I can't stay here." The memories of Olaus were everywhere. But she busied herself with daily activities, and soon a new feeling came over her. "It was almost as though this loved log house put its arms around me," she wrote. "There was warmth and purpose again."

Margaret knew that "the grief and the missing are never going to go away." She remembered, however, what her stepfather used to say whenever he was discouraged: "If you take one step with all the knowledge you have, there is usually enough light shining to show you the next step." She was determined to lead a happy life.

Margaret had reached an important decision. She would continue on her own the conservation work she had shared with Olaus for so many years. This was no time to sit on the sidelines. "Whatever happens," Margaret Murie insisted, "it's more fun to be in the performance than to stand with your face to the wall."

*"If we saved every scrap of wilderness . . .
it wouldn't be enough."*

Chapter 6

Saving the Wild Country

On a bright summer day in 1964, Margaret Murie sat in the Rose Garden of the White House. She was one of several conservationists who had been invited to witness a historic event. On this day, President Lyndon Johnson would sign the Wilderness Act, permanently placing nine million acres of forestland under government protection.

It had been a long struggle. Oil, mining, and timber companies objected strongly to the Wilderness Act. They would no longer be able to take natural resources from the protected areas to meet increasing demands for energy and building materials. Cattle ranchers also protested the loss of grazing lands for their herds.

But the Muries and other conservationists urged people to speak and write in favor of the law. "People say politicians don't read letters," said Margaret, "but I happen to know they *do*."

In 1966, Margaret published her second book, *Wapiti Wilderness* ("wapiti" is an Indian word for elk). Both Margaret and Olaus had worked on this colorful portrait of family life in the Wyoming wilderness. But Margaret was soon forced to turn her attention to the far-north region of her earlier years. In Alaska, conservationists were about to face one of their biggest challenges.

In 1968, a massive oil deposit was found on the North Slope of the Brooks Range, where Olaus had first studied the Alaskan caribou. The North Slope was a truly remote Arctic wilderness. Now, it, too, was threatened.

In 1973, despite the protests of environmentalists, the Alaska pipeline was built. It stretched across the entire state from Prudhoe Bay to the southern port of Valdez, a distance of 800 miles. From Valdez, the oil was shipped by ocean tanker to the West Coast of the United States.

To Margaret Murie, the pipeline was "the great black shadow over Alaska." But she also sensed that something positive had happened to the Alaskan people. The pipeline "brought about a change in their thinking," she wrote. "They see now how the land can be taken over and changed, and they are beginning to be truly concerned over what could happen to the land, to the future, the way of life of their children and their children's children."

After their failure to stop the pipeline, a number of local conservation groups combined to form the Alaska Coalition. Its members came from many backgrounds—including business as well as conservation groups. The coalition supported the establishment of protected wilderness areas and wildlife refuges in Alaska.

In 1975, the National Park Service appointed Murie as a consultant. She spent several weeks touring wilderness regions in Alaska. The government wanted to see if these areas should be included in the National Park System. Traveling by plane, Margaret visited several areas new to her, but there were trips to some familiar spots as well. In the village of Beetles, where she and Olaus had spent the first few weeks of their honeymoon, she visited their old cabin, now abandoned and in disrepair.

On this journey, Murie met with businesspeople and scientists, educators and tourists, park rangers and traders. Together, they discussed the impact on Alaska's wildlife of such issues as logging, commercial fishing, and oil prospecting. "I found a strong overall feeling that the wild untouched places of Alaska must be saved," Murie reported about the people she met. "They want this to happen, but they don't know who is going to do it or how an ordinary citizen can take part."

When her inspection of the proposed parklands was complete, Murie's conclusion was firm. "My sincere opinion is that each of these areas is outstandingly worthy of consideration as a National Park or National Monument," she informed the director of the Park Service.

At the end of her assignment, Murie returned to Wyoming to continue her conservation efforts. "The five weeks with the National Park Service in Alaska was one of the most deeply inspiring periods of my life," she wrote. "Let us hope we can inspire Congress also!"

In 1976, Murie attended a government committee hearing in Denver, Colorado, to support the Alaska Lands Act. The bill would do for Alaska what the Wilderness Act had done for areas in the "lower 48" states. More than a hundred million acres of wilderness would be permanently protected by the government.

When it was her turn to address the committee, Murie spoke from her heart. "I don't know whether the human race is going to survive very much longer; I sometimes wonder whether we deserve to," she said.

She argued that "saving the last remnants of wild untouched country" was the one course of action that the American people could take to preserve their own future. "Surely the United States of America is not so poor we cannot afford to have these places, not so rich that we can do without them.

"I have known Alaska all these years," Murie declared. "All Alaska needs to do is be Alaska."

Margaret Murie was now 73 years old. Her advice on important wilderness issues was sought by both legislators and conservationists. How can the timber industry conserve more forestland? How can the caribou be protected outside of state and national parklands? Should the wolf be allowed to flourish in Yellowstone National Park? What is the best way for conservation groups to communicate with local governments? These were some of the many questions posed to the "godmother" of the environmental movement.

It was four years before the work of Murie and many others insured that Alaska would be allowed to be Alaska. On December 2, 1980, President Jimmy Carter signed the Alaska Lands Act. The act established or enlarged 16 national wildlife refuges and 15 parks, monuments, and preserves. It also placed 24 Alaskan rivers under the protection of the National Wild and Scenic River System. A tremendous variety of wild animals and natural ecosystems (from forests to glaciers, from marshes to active volcanoes) were saved.

That same year, Margaret Murie received the Audubon Medal, one of the most prestigious awards of the environmental movement. The following year, 1981, Margaret Murie became the first woman to be given the

Sierra Club's John Muir Award. In 1986, the Wilderness Society presented her with the Robert Marshall Conservation Award.

But to Murie, her work itself is the most important reward—and there is much work to be done. The threat to the natural environment continues. In 1988, for instance, the fragile ecosystem of the Alaskan coast was endangered when the oil tanker *Exxon Valdez* struck an underwater reef. Millions of gallons of oil were washed upon the shore, killing animals and polluting wildlife habitats.

For Margaret Murie, such an environmental tragedy must serve as a warning of the dangers that face the American wilderness. "If we saved every scrap of wilderness we have," she says, "it wouldn't be enough."

Chapter 7

Teaching About the Wilderness

Today, at over age 90, Margaret Murie remains active in the fight to save the wilderness. Her family continues to be an important part of Murie's life, too, and although her three children and ten grandchildren live in different areas of the country, she makes frequent trips to visit them. Her sister Louise lives close by in Jackson Hole, Wyoming. A typical afternoon finds the two women exploring the surrounding woods on cross-country skis.

Murie continues to be curious about the natural world around her. "If you're curious enough about life and what's in it," she believes, you're always striving to learn more. "I've always said that curiosity can keep you going when everything else fails."

According to Murie, it was curiosity that drove Olaus to endure the hardship of the Alaskan wilderness. "He had a very dedicated and keen curiosity about everything that ever walked or crawled or lived," Murie says. "That was his motivating force—to find out more. He used to say that there is no limit to man's capacity to learn things, if man didn't destroy himself first by destroying his earth."

Murie's home is also the headquarters for her public life. She still writes letters and makes phone calls to members of Congress, supporting new legislation to protect wilderness areas and wildlife habitats. She doesn't have to look far to be reminded of the importance of her cause. Bear, moose, and deer are a few of the animals that make the forest around her cabin their home. A family of furry martens regularly visits her kitchen door for scraps of food.

The cabin has its share of human visitors, too. When conservationists come together in the area, they usually decide to hold a meeting at her cabin. "Why not?" asks Margaret. "I want my home to go on being used in this way." The conservationists agree that they would rather "sit in front of the fireplace and eat carrot cake" than meet downtown.

In spite of continuing threats to America's wilderness areas, Murie remains confident about the future. She is convinced that young people share her concern about the preservation of wild places.

For Margaret Murie, the chance to see these places, to know the wonder of nature—this is a right that people should claim. "For those of us who feel something is missing unless we can hike across land disturbed only by our footsteps or see creatures roaming freely as they have always done, we are sure there should still be wilderness."

On a sunny summer day, Margaret Murie awaits a group of students making the hike to her cabin. It is time for another nature lesson. More than 80 years have passed since Murie began her own wilderness education. And the lessons that she learned she happily passes on to future generations.

For Margaret Murie, preserving the wilderness is an obligation that we have to others. It is a debt, according to Murie, that we owe to the future:

> I've had enough experiences for twelve lifetimes. So I feel that the least I can do is to try to save what little we have left for the future. I know a lot of young people will appreciate this country, if given a chance. But they can't if the country isn't there. It all comes back to what things we think are important in life.

Glossary

biologist   a person who studies the science of living things

caribou   a deer of arctic regions

conservation   the process by which natural resources are saved

ecosystem   the network of relationships among living things and their environment

elk   a large deer that lives in northern regions and has antlers

environment   the physical world that surrounds a plant or animal

environmental movement   the activities of a group of people working for the protection of the environment

evergreen   a tree or plant that has green leaves that remain all year

glacier   a large formation of ice capable of movement

grouse   a chubby bird of the Northern Hemisphere having gray or brown speckled feathers

habitat	an area or environment in which a plant or animal normally lives
inlet	a bay or cove along the coast that often leads inward away from the ocean or flows between two islands
mushing	travel over snow with a sled pulled by dogs
peninsula	a long extension of land into water
predator	an animal that survives by preying upon others
range	an extensive area of land; a chain of mountains
ranger	a person employed to inspect and protect a certain area
specimen	a sample of something for study
sternwheel steamer	a steamboat propelled by a rear wheel that has boards or paddles around its circumference
tundra	a treeless area in arctic regions found between the ice cap and the tree line
varmint	an animal or bird considered a pest
volcano	a mountain formed by the flow of lava and gases from a crack in the earth's crust

wilderness an area of land left in its natural condition

wildlife animals or plants living in a natural state

wildlife a place or area of land providing
refuge protection for wild animals and plants

Index